"Kristofer Collins brilliantly captures what life has been like in our fractured country in these pandemic years where we've been left wondering how to redeem meaning from the political rubble, and how to go forth with eyes open- even while sometimes teetering on the edge of despair. Despite his wrestling with a dark time, Collins ultimately offers us a vision where friendship and love become even more crucial. So many poems here are addressed to specific people, and you come away remembering that our connection to one another is what sustains us, as does our loyalty to place- in this case Pittsburgh- not quite "a fountain city" as his two year old son believes, but a hard won turf brimming with history and memory. "Is someone in that silent house hurting?" he wonders in "Music", the question illuminating Collins' desire to extend the already wide net of his compassion. His distinctive, unpretentious voice makes him the sort of poet who feels like a trusted friend you want to carry with you as you make your way home."

-Jane McCafferty, author of *Thank You for the Music*

"Reading a Kristofer Collins poem is like having a stranger ask to share your table in a coffee shop and, two hours later, walking away with a thoughtful new friend. Or reading a Collins poem is like sidling up to your oldest pal in a quiet bar and talking about the ordinary stuff of your day in transcendent ways. Or maybe reading a Collins poem is like taking a winter walk with the best and most tuned-in version of yourself, that part of you who knows deeply the world's darkness, but in the darkness, still insists on light. Pick your metaphor, but these breathlessly unspooling, wonderfully grounded poems about our interdependence will remind you "sometimes we get lucky and don't have to spend all/ those tumbling hours alone."

-Nancy Krygowski, author of *The Woman in the Corner*

"*Roundabout Trace* is at once elegiac and alive with the restless music of nostalgia for what our cities and our country once were, and for who we once were. Though brief, Collins' poems are full-bodied, brimming with frank and precise language and stirring imagery. Pittsburghers especially will find much to savor in this timely collection."

-Deesha Philyaw, author of *The Secret Lives of Church Ladies*

"*Roundabout Trace* is a deep dive into the playful, but always profound consciousness of a poet who never retreats into metaphysical mumbo-jumbo to make a point. This is a collection of poems that is at times droll, laugh out loud funny, morally serious, imagistic and always connected to the real world. I can see, smell, taste and touch the things Collins writes about in this brilliant collection. Kristofer Collins has been the dean of poetry critics in Pittsburgh for years. With *Roundabout Trace*, he can take his place at the head of the table of major local poets Michael Wurster has kept warm for him."

-Tony Norman is a columnist and book review editor for the *Pittsburgh Post-Gazette*

"Kristofer Collins is descended from James Wright, Edgar Lee Masters, Edwin Arlington Robinson and Waylon Jennings – American elegists who lament not only the dead, but also the death of illusion. Collins casts a cold eye on our post-industrial republic of collapsing bridges, crumbling streets, boarded up storefronts, "flayed men on unemployment" and "The homes of friends blackened/ by despair." He takes his listener into the depths of our national nightmare, and then, like any great elegist, lifts us into love: "in the way/ the vibrations of guitar strings mirrored/ our vibrating bodies." And eventually, into hope: "the years rolling out/ in front of me a tender invitation/ to stick around."

-Michael Simms, author of *American Ash* and *Nightjar*

Roundabout Trace

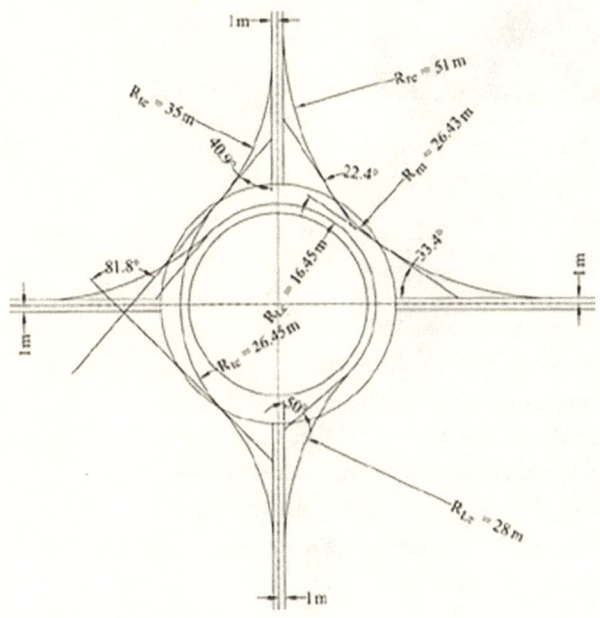

Poems 2019-2022

by

Kristofer Collins

Kung Fu Treachery Press
Rancho Cucamonga, CA

Copyright © 2022, Krstofer Collins

First Edition: 1 3 5 7 9 10 8 6 4 2

ISBN: 978-1-958182-06-2

LCCN: 2022940186

Author photo: Kristofer Collins

Cover image: *McSorley's Bar* by John French Sloan, courtesy of the Detroit Institute of Arts.

Acknowledgments:

Grateful acknowledgment is made to the publications *Appalachian Lit, Jerry Jazz Musician, Vox Populi,* and *Winedrunk Sidewalk* for giving some of the poems here very fine homes indeed.

With endless thanks and appreciation to everyone at Roundabout Brewery and Trace Brewing for providing the welcoming spaces in which these poems were written.

Special thanks to Jason Irwin, Scott Silsbe, and Michael Simms for fresh eyes and sparkling encouragement while this book came together.

With gratitude and appreciation to Jason Ryberg and John T. Keehan, Jr..

Eternal love and gratitude to my family for their patience and support.

TABLE OF CONTENTS

A Poem for Michael Wurster / 1

Music / 2

Neighborhoods / 3

Small Town Romance / 4

Out of This Country / 5

Pat Martino at The Balcony / 6

Miles Davis Comes to Lawrenceville / 7

On Reading Tomas Tranströmer in an
    Election Year / 8

Vigil / 9

Gene's Last Chance / 10

Close Motion / 11

On Listening to the Bee Gees' Massachusetts
    Late One Evening / 12

Magnolia Clock Co., Magnolia, TX at
    Ka-Fair Coffee, Pgh, PA / 13

Jack Teagarden Buries Louis Armstrong's
    Oriental Strut, Mesa NM, ca.1926 / 14

Good Days / 16

Fountain City / 17

Poem for Luke Kuzmish / 19

49th & Blackberry Way / 20

Blackberry Way / 21

Red Tables / 22

Early November Poem with Drunken Mosquito / 23

Looking at the Lake / 24

Quit This Town / 25

Poem for Brian Broome / 26

Good Time Charlie's Got the Blues / 28

The Girl with the White Boots / 29

Bridget / 31

A Poem for Jude Vachon / 32

Why Write Poems? / 33

One More Body / 34

Lost Signals / 35

December 5, 2021 / 36

Schubert / 37

A Last Beer Before Heading Home / 38

The Midtown Yacht Club / 39

Jimmy Tsang's / 40

Ode to Dr. Sestric's Office / 41

Uneeda Biscuit / 42

January / 43

Sarah / 44

Beer for Breakfast / 45

A Letter to Jeffrey Dunn 1/21/22 / 46

Paddy Cake / 48

Forgotten Works / 49

Poem for a Friend in February / 50

Tommy Flanagan Plays Billy Strayhorn's Daydream,
    Tokyo, 2/15/75 / 51

City Steps 2/26/22 / 52

Poem for Scott Silsbe / 53

The Couple to Our Left / 54

Coffee Cups from the Kitchen / 55

Scotty's Diner / 56

Roundabout Trace / 57

I Like It Here / 58

Poem / 68

In Memory of
Jude Vachon
&
Tami LaRoche

(I)n a nation that is no longer one but only an amorphous collection of failed dreams, where we have been told too often by contractors, corporations and prudes that our lives don't matter, there still is a place where the soul doesn't recognize laws like gravity...

-Richard Hugo, from *Letter to Oberg from Pony*

O friends, no more these sounds!
Let us sing more cheerful songs,
more full of joy!

-Friedrich Von Schiller, from *Ode to Joy*

Roundabout Trace

A Poem for Michael Wurster

Michael Wurster once said everyone should write
a poem about a steel mill, but the mills
were relics even when I was a boy; the red,
hot pump of this town gone cool and quiet
long before my first kiss. And now that this once
shy sun has revealed itself as a white disc,
clean and ascendant above the grit and haze
watching the motions of the city, why
memorialize the mills? I write mostly of bars,
and sometimes the rivers. Maybe

there is no magic left to the mills. The infernal
roar, the colossal burn that made a dull knife
of the air. The only connection I felt to the mills
was to the children of a generation of flayed men
on unemployment, the storefronts boarded, the city
emptied. The homes of friends blackened
by despair and made dangerous by depression,
alcoholism, and irrevocable violence.

Since then I have climbed the shadowy bulk
of Carrie Furnace, imagined the deafening blaze,
and took note of each weed now sprouted
where the heavy-shod feet of lonely men
pressed a signature of sorts into the poisoned ground.

So here, Michael, after too many years is the poem
promised your sincere exhortation. Here, finally,
is more air incapacitated with ash. More water
you'd be a fool to drink. Here is a poem
to melt the ground on which you stand.

Music

The music is always dying
and so, I'm afraid, is everything
else. I attend funerals too often,
and those mostly for ideas

like empathy and common concern.
What are the neighbors up to?
Do I even care? Is someone
in that silent house hurting? Up there

in the bedroom, how many pills
fill that rigid fist? Today the
president called himself
the chosen one, and the rest of us

just shrugged. All the buildings
have blown down on Butler St.
The cemetery trees were yanked
out at the roots and thrown

by an invisible hand
at the graves, as if to say
Hey you dead, get ready.
There's company coming.

Neighborhoods

I guess you'd call me a fool spending an afternoon
at home and without a solitary beer, the white
cat tailless and yowling at every leaf blowing
across the yard, the cicadas have punched
the clock early and, patiently as tinsmiths, work
the heavy air into song. The neighbor woman
finally went insane and shut herself in the vacant
chicken coop collapsing into the hillside.
That helicopter still patrols the neighborhood hoping
to, but not finding any of our lost children.
So little has changed. Perhaps on an errand I stop
in some public room and greet you like a friend.
More often I stare at my hands in shame. Would it
surprise you to learn I dreamt of you again last
night? In my dreams your hair is auburn and long
like it never was. In my dream this city grows new
neighborhoods like hearts dripping from some fairy
tale tree. I move through them a stranger watching
for familiar eyes. I expect great things, but the
disappointment hardly matters. This is what I will tell
my son, should he ever be found.

Small Town Romance

You could almost weep for the bankrupt bartender,
but watching his hands for a sign of mercy
is the very definition of a wasted day. Over the
entrance they've hung a sign that insists you go away.
Habit is the law of the land. Pride and prurience
are rewarded, just as empathy is openly despised.
They'll piss on you just as soon as leave you dead,
translates the Latin on our family crest. Get out
the shovel there's another truth we need to bury.
That old couple shares the window table every day
about this time, the blood softly clanking around
their gray bodies. He worked a double as often as he could
and she did the same. So went youth and dreams.
The streets are crumbling and our chief exports are cancer
and cruelty. Lately we've all gone unlisted in the phone
directory. Blank pages like a thing a ghost would write.

Out of This Country

Talking only to myself under the shuddering lights
of the YMCA, the Mexican War Streets storm into
the perilous evening. Somewhere my son is grinning
and getting ready to yell. I feel as though I could
collapse on some manicured stoop and with little
effort disappear into the dust. The park must be
some battlefield where the ghosts of our failures
stalk one another, the blood of good intentions
staining the ground. A few bucks and here's a bourbon
poured neat. A few more and now I'm surrounded
by new friends. Where will it all lead? With a fool
in the White House all things are possible. Every
manner of humiliation right there at my fingertips.
Say you are lost, this will bind you to the rest of us.
Out of this valley there is a chance at a better life.
Out of this city, out of this state. Out of this country.
It's a time for sad truths. This is the best life I could
hope for. The same could be said of you. Don't let
it be said of you.

Pat Martino at The Balcony

That night we caught Pat Martino
at The Balcony I want to say
it was raining, and there was still
some love between us, in the way
the vibrations of guitar strings mirrored
our vibrating bodies, eyes falling
on one another like strangers,
like something seen from so great a distance
it could be the shadow of many birds,
or the absence of what we once pledged;
perhaps when he played the Sondheim tune
we finally saw each failure crystallized
like a museum artifact we would visit
Sundays separately and for no other reason
than once many years ago it seemed
the most beautiful of wonders, a jewel
in whose heart the rain was perpetual,
the thrum of it quivering against
my nerves, humming up and down
the bright window of your throat.

Miles Davis Comes to Lawrenceville

for John Grochalski

You remember the blade of his horn
running that voodoo down, driving
the lank end of Butler St.
somewhere in the ugly weeds
of your twenties, the haloed refinery

tankers rampant on the river's edge,
and Grochalski at the wheel while
somewhere out in the cracked night
a girl waited, swarmed in want.

The silence of those tankers, big and white
as Polish butchers, blood in the drab
folds of their skin, haunts this music now.

Mournful as the plain gray sentences
of ghosts, the steps shattered
snaking up our shared hills, we felt
the accumulated loneliness of parishioners
and widows exiting St. Augustine's.

The sky was a grid straining to find
some looser language, some mute cry
absent of recrimination.

The cool shade of night drawing down
on our desire, one last exhalation
weary of the wish for redemption.

On Reading Tomas Tranströmer
in an Election Year

At first it's only my eyes I feel
dripping down the lines and pooling
somewhere west of Stockholm, a blaze
of traffic over my shoulder and still
this glassy puddle underfoot, the blades
and engines writhing again at the river,
and my pen too, now angry in the dense
rending noise. The chimneys stark
and blowing hate into the February sky,
like a sheet draped across a still face.
The music I hear full of nothing. Lines
of it blown on the air, clear as gas, no less
than a signature of sighs. Try to make sense
of it. These words suddenly a creeping
thing. They wait in the woods for more
like you. Their faces burnt in shame, flush
cheeks daubed bloody by the only world we knew

Vigil

for William Taylor, Jr.

On her third cigarette, alone and no one here
has the heart to say put it out so we drink
alone in our own ways and hook theses wishes
to the white tails of her breath and watch
Golden State move the ball without pause
but not really watching, but slowly and quietly each
one here fits new locks on the doors we're closing
ourselves behind. Later I'll slip Chopin's
Nocturnes on the turntable and listen to these
other locks sliding open with each little touch.
Later still I'll dream of those four o'clock winds
crashing my body as the late sun wavered
querulously over San Francisco and I'll tell
myself I loved there, I was loving and loved
and even later still I will see this reflection only
slightly recognizable as mine ghosting the window
as little pink fingers of morning grip the edge
of the East End and I'll know all at once
the many lies I've been telling myself since then.

Gene's Last Chance

for Scott Silsbe

Pity Gene for washing up here
dry as no August ever was
in Pittsburgh, scorched and sanded
of tongue and bereft of options.
Pity us for stinginess and never throwing
a solitary die and trying our luck.
I heard the rotgut came equipped
with a fresh razor blade tucked
in the shallow well of each shot,
sleek as a fish under the mud.
There to satisfy that final urge.
Anyway, I remember we talked
about rolling in one night
to sample the sauce, but on
spying the sparse parking lot
kept on going, not ready
to call it quits and join old Gene
in the gullet of oblivion, this city
still a siren out there singing
so strangely, and that song still
something we needed to hear.

Close Motion

for Bart & Tami

I guess we'll have to wait
another year for our promise
to share the waters off
Cape Ann, to stare at Fitz Henry
Lane's luminist Brace's Rock
then set ourselves to the real
thing. Gloucester decked
in shards of oyster shells and brine,
the girth of Olson roundly guffawing
at my poems and barking outside
the door to heaven a bedeviled,
Wow!, his head shaking loose
a pelting of lice and wild laughter.
The moon closer now, our bodies
blood-warm and glowing
in the tide's retreat; our mouths
released and all that we contain
mingling into the lives of tourists,
fishermen, and the shared chaos
of all these bodies in close motion.

On Listening to the Bee Gees' Massachusetts
Late One Evening

I touch your hand to see what will happen
same as I walk the broken face of Penn
Avenue or the bent sweep of the 31st Street
Bridge, the worry piling up faster than
the wonder, no illusions but newly desperate
for some hopeful sign. I pass the far end
of Butler Street and sometimes cross
the 62nd Street Bridge by bus, looking for beer
or groceries, sometimes overwhelmed
by the memory of a shared pizza and the tense
set of everyone's eyes watching the game
in overtime. Sometimes not even sun or rain
just a sound like an engine kicking into gear
then dying. And when I'm alone and crossing
the Bloomfield Bridge I feel the shuddering,
hear the ghosts of sirens, my grandparents
with no time to pack a single bag, the train
derailed, chemicals frying into the overcast
air. And then on those nights you leave,
I watch storms settle in their purple rags
over the river, and the radio is playing
this song my father loved; the burnt ozone
falling out of us, this withered love
we have nowhere to put, the voices
walking out of the music are not here
to help, they don't even see us,
these hearts they happily break.

Magnolia Clock Co. Magnolia, TX at Ka-Fair Coffee, Pgh, PA

It makes no sense this clock bigger than
the wall it hangs on. It really is the state
of Texas come here to crowd us all out
onto Chislett Street, just another herd of steer
delivered to slaughter. The ticking loud
as an argument, loud as two lovers
angry in their fucking, and angrier
in their sleep. I came here as a kid
for haircuts, one of the few things I did
with my dad. I'd stare at the red boil
fastened to Porco's forearm as the clippers
chewed up my neck. Bob & Kay's
was the candy store over there, now
a dentist's office. Hours I spent in the back
for a root canal, the whole time tasting
Swedish Fish on my tongue. I played in pick-up
games here. In the multipurpose room
at St. Raphael's I danced my first slow dance
with Dina Conti. I said I'd never come back.
This clock calls bullshit on that kid I was.
So do I. Morningside is eternal, or maybe
only inescapable. My days are fewer now
by many. That candy I came here for
never did taste right.

Jack Teagarden Buries Louis Armstrong's Oriental Strut, Mesa, NM, ca.1926

for Nancy Krygowski

Nancy, I'm writing you from here in the year of everything
falling apart, where Jack Teagarden sings the oldest blues
he ever heard on the radio, where half of this August sky
is smudged with rain and the rest is simply too tired to try,
and where the voices of old friends sound distant and frail
like a thing wounded and struggling in the ditch, gone to
ground in the fresh mud whispering names of the no longer
living, and then all too soon the voices are gone as well leaving
only the mourning dove perched over the street lamenting
in my ear, and then the breeze is picking up, warm on my
neck like a damp washcloth, and everywhere around
is just more loneliness attired in familiar shapes, the shadows
the blowing leaves throw around mirror these intricate webs
of blood vessels crowding the loose skin sunk beneath
the eyes of some other old man awash in light and loss,
and lifting the tarnished curve of his horn to papery lips, Jack
Teagarden somewhere in 1947, his heart piled up with booze
and debt, but still a suppleness to his mouth, a flash
of something dangerous in the hard set of his jaw, something
finally empty of tears, and here as the breath rises he is again
a young man kicking the desert dust of Mesa, NM, ca.1926,
the sky here unchiseled by itinerant clouds but still cruel in
its cherished adolescence and far, with his knees in the sun-
packed dirt, his hands become trowels, the bones in his
fingers breaking the ground, gouging something greater
than a grave into the land, here to bury this fragile shellac,
this bright utterance from the uncageable soul, he believes

will now outlast all of America, this fossil-to-be locked under
the hard earth, jubilant souls in glory, never silent, forever
there should we need the reminder, Nancy, that such things
matter, the very best of us will last long after the worst
of everything is only a shameful memory.

Good Days

Today has been easier, both heat
and rain stayed away leaving
only the lightest of breezes
and a cooler of beer for company
as I watch the neighbors and wave
from the porch, the hill tumbling
over itself in somersaults
of overgrown grass, the songs
of barking dogs and snorting deer,
the syncopation of squirrels
tapping across the tin roof. I could drink
beer after beer and never fear anything
worse than a lovely mild buzz.
My place in this life a given
and the years rolling out
in front of me a tender invitation
to stick around, so many good days
coming still.

Fountain City

for Tami LaRoche

Tami, my son is exuberant in his two-year old's
jabberwocky telling me about the peek-a-boo
fountain he visited with his grandparents
downtown, a clockwork splashing of shooting
jets leaping in counterpoint from the stony plaza.
It's made an impression. So has what he calls
The Big Fountain, its triumphant celebratory
spray swatting the juicy fat wedge of The Point.
Then there's the messy irregularity of the North Side
fountain he dips his toes in and cups tiny red handfuls
from weekly. My son believes this is a fountain city,
an exquisite conglomeration of bubbling, bursting
liquid, the cool spray a constant sign of our shared kindness.
Tami, who am I to tell him no? Today is that rare day
of being on my own. Even in this national nightmare
I can still, if only this Wednesday afternoon, slide myself
safely at some distance into a small, outdoor table, order
a beer among strangers while waiting for the bus to come,
and here with the can of domestic popped and almost
gone I watch the water gurgling like a newborn
in this courtyard that once was a funeral home.
The whole country looks like a funeral home now, Tami,
decked in ancient shag carpeting and flaking paint,
all of us walking numb, greeting each other in whispers
as if offering condolences, which in fact we are, our eyes
never leaving the ground, and if they do for a flicker
they jump right back to the safety of the floor and to
the coronal edge of our ever-present masks. Tami, I don't call

this music what the water is doing. Not a song, not even
a voice. But for the moment it is the sound of something
straining to live, noisy and as gloriously careless
as a two-year old stumbling and burbling and clutching
the air like he owns it, like it's his due and everything
he could ever desire from this world, and it is also the sound
of welcome, a cacophony of bells oceanic announcing
the arrival of a much-loved and long-missed guest, here finally
to remind us of who we were in those days when we knew
what was truly precious, and what the sip of something cool,
the touch of that coolness against our callused bodies,
how it lifted our spirits and so unselfishly gave us
this gift of each other. Tami, I was just here missing you
and I wanted you to know.

Poem for Luke Kuzmish

"You poor bastard," says Luke,
"what are you doing in Erie?
Come over. I have my kid
for the weekend. I'll make some chili."
And I can almost smell those red
beans bubbling as I sit here
in this rehabbed train station,
ghosts of engines still smoking
in the garden as I wave for another
and the bartender admits, embarrassed,
"I don't read so much as I want."
The old man in his Huntin' Bucks,
Drivin' Trucks t-shirt adds what's left
of his lungs to a yellow-stained hanky
and somehow I just know Chuck Joy
is dancing the hoochy-koo at Poet's Hall.
A day wasted at The Whippy Dip and
the racks of a Salvation Army behind me
I want nothing but to sink into the foam
and the air conditioned murk. Einstein on the Beach
falling out of the radio and sea gulls dropping
into the dumpster. I found a hundred dollar bill
on my walk here and thought, Drugs.
Who's to say what is right in a post-give-a-damn
country. What's the point of worrying now
we're past the threshold and all this flesh
and the love that pounded at it is out there
on the lake burning a hole into heaven, a place
as empty as any other dying town.

49th & Blackberry Way

How did we arrive here? One day
bumping elbows at the bar with a
heavy-coated man hunkered over a pile
of oily greens, the cherry tomatoes lighting
up his plate like firecrackers, and the next
I'm pitching brown empties into the crisp cemetery
grass trying to remember the opening riff to Ripple,
instead humming Chopin's Piano Sonata No. 2.
Did I mistakenly follow some black bird refusing
to believe how gladly it had tied itself to death?
Here where we have to hide our shortness of breath,
it's merely amazement at this historical moment
that makes me gasp. I really thought we'd make it
to the end, maybe a few pints low on blood, sure, but
then only shaken by the chill feeling rendered unto
our bones by weekend grave walkers; how they whistle
all the beautiful tunes and how we hate
them for the ease with which they leave us crying in the dirt.

Blackberry Way

A book of poems, pint
of beer, Zombo's old house
looking fine in the March
sunshine; Dyana pours
another clad in black,
the traffic almost calling
her name like a dozen lovers
knees bent in the pot-holed
rubble, eyes dipped
in the fresh dew
of this still new year.

Red Tables

Red tables empty
in the sun
birdsong, blue sky
and all the rest.
Over the cemetery
gate there's a turning
in the graves
same as the leaves
of scattered maples,
the dead inviting the rain
down for a friendly
word.

Early November Poem with Drunken Mosquito

A forecast of snow
means we'll pack
the porch furniture
away and light the last
of the citronella,
these famished things
all over the air, they're
stupid for our blood;
jumping right from
this fresh bite a-drip
on my knuckle one
of the bastards bombs
into my last swallow
of beer gulping
the golden pool while
I'm left to suck
the red wet from my
finger; neither myself
nor the mosquito
getting what we wanted
out of the day.

Looking at the Lake

for Jude Vachon

Fresh cords of wood stacked against
the eastward wall and some songs
I knew all the words to in high school
add their old crackle to the fire's
static; the empty courtyard
and the black-bricked Chinese restaurant
beyond get hazy at the edges, grow
soft as mud. I could use a drink,
but I was sick all last night, so
I drink my water from this blue cup
instead. All the words I know, each one
a useless thing. I think of your ashes
in a small jelly jar on a shelf in the pantry
at home, useless too. Where are your
wonderful ideas now? All ten thousand
of them, each one a tiny grain you
let loose in this world. I should have done
more, I guess. Should maybe have said
something. I don't know what language
could have reached you out there
on the lake, what bridge could be bothered
to bring you back now.

Quit This Town

The maps on the wall all suggest
I could, in fact, be somewhere else.
A beach on the coast of New Zealand
say, or Ybor City if I like. Just go
somewhere. Why not? Hell, if I look
out the window there is the sun, not
an expected companion this late
into a week of mid-August thunder
storms. If I imagined myself one
of those billionaires I could arrange
to have myself shot straight into
the heart of that star, shimmering
down hot rays composed of my blood
and semen, showering these vast
continents with my superlative DNA.
Or over the gated wall into the tree-shaded,
goose-shit littered greenery of Allegheny
Cemetery, and with a blade of grass
hung on my lip I would taste that pure
vintage of fear and regret, barrel-aged
in its way since the 1840s. Flaubert
did say, Travel makes you modest
after all and what better to offer perspective
than infinite space and the endless dead.
Whether to the sun or simply crossing Butler
Street it's all the same. Whatever sadness
is there in your bones walks every step
with you, whispering What does it matter,
What does it matter.

Poem for Brian Broome

My father, sitting somewhere in Ohio,
idly sips his wine while my mother,
who lives three doors down from me,
worries the cancer has come back,
perhaps now it has moved to her kidneys,
and the roof, too, on her house showing its age.
My parents both coursing in me like one
long rolling street known by two different names.
Sure, this is Craig Street, but it's Billy Conn
Blvd too. Talking Heads played a pizza
joint down here, and couldn't Brando himself
have been another Billy Conn. So said
Rod Steiger, andwe hear Elia Kazan call cut
and Eva Marie Saint walks into a bar called
The Holiday on Christmas Eve, the man
pouring drinks looks just like the Newark
of her youth, and some other Pittsburgh
kid, this one called Andy, supposedly
hid a mural under all this muck on the walls.
The Christmas lights here blinking and me
sipping some kind of mix of every fruit
liqueur in the joint, that's the holiday special.
Only a little sweeter than what Steve jokingly
pours me some nights at the BBT. It's a sipper,
not a shooter, he always winks. These doors
all folding closed in the junkyard of memories
so filled up with movies and rumors, my body
loud with the competing noise of my parents,
my nerves wired to this city as a flash comes

across the sky and the lights all go out and
in the hot-cold dark a quiet comes up and
wraps its arms around me from behind like
Billy Strayhorn reaching out for Lena Horne
that time he ripped the music from the rivers
and called it by all our names, my name too
sitting there like some scared thing, loose sand
along the water's edge too easily sucked under.

Good Time Charlie's Got the Blues

for Richard Gegick

Hey Rich, I was just here thinking
of that time at Gooski's when Suspicious
Minds came on the juke and a girl
who kept turning up, bad penny-like,
let rip this huge guffaw, one I'd heard
in other bars on other nights and once
on the North Side at some punk
show, a laugh she must have gotten
from her dad, some proud and slightly
embarrassing inheritance, but hell this
thing boomed around the bar, like a bomb
gone off, man, and I never did get a glimpse
of that girl but I loved her. That laugh
would shatter me, impale my atoms
to the wall, ache me quake me, you know,
and I'd pop my head up like a goddamned
rocket and scan the scene, desperate-like,
where is she?, never did catch sight
of her, but I know she sure was there,
somewhere in the smoke and noise,
and Timmy behind the bar, or Larry
pouring us another pitcher, and Elvis, too,
he was there back in the kitchen deep-frying
chicken wings, slinging pierogis, hot butter
all over the place, all over his chin, coz he
drank that shit straight, and crying the whole
time, his mother gone more than half a century
and he's still gutted by the knowledge
that he is truly and forever alone and nothing
funny about it.

The Girl with the White Boots

for Scott Silsbe

There's a girl here with a white belt on drinking
beer reminding me of the girl with white boots
you wanted to write a country song about, who
cracked herself into your dreams, into your
language, filling her body into your fingers
as you laughed and strummed your guitar
ala Hank Williams, no cowboy hat but sure
you'd been putting down pints like it would score
you a slot at the Opry; and maybe that night we
were at Duke's Place, maybe at the old spot
Lou would eventually buy, long before Lou
laid it all out on a dream and that goddamned
giant shark he stuck to the wall like a grinning
sword of Damocles dangling scarily over the
back corner booth; and maybe all our dreams
are really just sharks looking for the easy kill, hoping
the girl comes along to save your life, inspire a
great song or a mediocre poem, or maybe
it's all a scam we sell ourselves just to get going
every day and not jump that bridge Jakiela's
always on about, and root ourselves in the now,
fully hopeful that love might be real and we ourselves
real too in some meaningful way; and some night
some kid turns on the radio (do kids still listen
to radios?) and there she is – white boots, white
belt, a woman full of hurt and joy, a whole world,
woman of constant mystery – and that kid finally
intersects with a kind of love and that's thanks to you;

and maybe after that, down the road years and years,
her body rests against another and in that moment,
and maybe only that moment she understands
herself as pure song, an awkward music of dreams
built and dashed as many times as she had the strength,
as someone secretly dreamed of by a stranger, and
touching her warm hand to her sleeping love, exhales
a white, hot breath, invisible and scorching, a song
unto the stars.

Bridget

This woman walking in the haze and sun
could be you, has a face that sets my brain
buzzing with shame. There's not much
in these intervening years, more than thirty,
I could point to with the conviction that I
have grown as a person. If you'd like
a guided tour of failure, however, I could
certainly oblige. Maybe it's the same
for you. Would you cover my folded hands
with yours and speak of alcoholism,
bankruptcy, or suicide? Would you offer God's
good news in exchange for an hour and coffee?
Do you still only read novels about talking
animals; still wear fizzy pink sweaters and pick
your nose? On solitary walks across the 40th
Street Bridge do you feel the pull of the churning
water below? Small fishing boats and tugs
drifting aimlessly, the river hard at their hulls
calling to them out of pure boredom. How full
the water must be; how like our own tumbling
bodies. Bridget, the day is coming when only
the Allegheny will speak well of us.

A Poem for Jude Vachon

The dry bones of autumn trees
wave down, splinters of sun shake
out from the sky. I will try hard
not to arouse the many possible
disasters at play out here. Tread
lightly, they say. Today I am left
this job of accounting. A shared
tally of mutual loss. Staring at
the stained asphalt I wonder
what you saw watching the loose
unbuckling of small waves
your last time at the lake. Your
one-time words crawl
into absences greater than the
note you never left. What
the hell were you thinking? Jude,
this world is all we have left.

Why Write Poems?

Why write poems?
Why watch from dark
corners of shitty
punk clubs drenched
in winter sweat, dancing
in heavy wool coats
with girlfriends I still
see around and still
love? Why bother
making sense of it?
I keep a box of old
letters in my closet
to remind myself
of the kinder man
I was. I hope
my son reads them
someday and understands
his father as someone
who cared and mattered
very much to a handful
of excellent people.
None of it lasted, but
for a short time
it was true.

One More Body

With practiced snap of the wrist
I dispose of one more body;
unfortunate this vole
to encounter our cat at 3am
in the winter-brittle weeds.
One more dead thing
to add to the pile
growing down the hillside,
deliquescing into moonlight
and mud. I stand here
watching clouds rimmed
in the coiled light, the star-born
fuzz and Venus giving me
the hairy eyeball. Another
season of urgent seclusion
is coming. Will we even remember
the rough texture of the loving
embrace? Reduced to muffled
voices and anonymous eyes
how do we expect to survive?
I'll sit out here the rest of the night
and won't feel the cold. Who can
honestly say they feel much of anything
anymore. My god, look at what we do.

Lost Signals

The music too loud is a tip-off
the barkeep doesn't want me
here. But what of my gorgeous
smile? Surely it melts your heart.
Instead I stop off for a six-pack,
drink some in the empty parking
lot behind the shuttered Goodwill.
A cat here, black-striped and mangy
in its Machiavellian affections.
Eventually I will return to an empty
house, the living-room light little
more than lost signals dispersed
across this loneliness. Looking
for a good country song on the radio,
there's little comfort in my success.
Who will hold me tonight as my body
shakes? Who will say, Someday
we will all be of the air, of night
and song? As if to say, Our absence
is what finally makes us beautiful.

December 5, 2021

Vague unease; morning's collapsing
gravity. Brake lights violent
in the ether. Last night's whiskey,
it's creeping red fingers linger
at the rim of one drooping eye.
No one stops at the Community
Market. The bars won't open
early enough for the bored men
at the bus stop. At least the smoke
shop trade is keeping up, crumpled
butts all around the door. A nervous trail
of them all the way to the Thai place
at the corner. I'll stop for coffee,
wait these things out. Shot through
with time, same as these old buildings.
One more crumbling thing, one more
memory left to the rain.

Schubert

It's not enough
not to be stupid.
Think of Schubert
brilliant, syphilitic,
almost entirely obscure;
held up by friends,
loved and invisible
tickling the ivories
at secret parties,
eyes erupting, lost
in his song. His bones
sugar this earth. So
clever. We still breathe
his atoms with the
summer dust.

A Last Beer Before Heading Home

So here I am still making slow work
of a pint while from the window
December is besotted of its own
depressive grays. I've lost track
of the unleashed dogs lifting
a hind leg in salute to the forlorn
strand of trees bent from the brash
windy push. This cussed stubbornness
of days, this slow rolling out
of an intricate worry, mirrors the coal-smear
of crows cracking hard beaks against
the weather. Orson Welles once said,
Our songs will all be silenced. Over there
so many names have melted into stone. Today
the lost choir is five million and counting.
Yet the bright orange flash of a family of foxes
carves its own space into the stillness.
But what of it, said Welles. Go on singing.

The Midtown Yacht Club

for Anna

We spent our time there praising the house-made
chips and re-fried beans, agog at the old couple.
She in white gloves, him with one foot
firmly planted in his great reward. An air of church
about them, and the bar dark as a sacristy.
The warm light of television toasted the bartender's
backside, while next door a little man in brogues
and sweater vest oiled the slide on some kid's
trombone. Up in Washington Park the book fair
is going on. Pages blowing in the fresh harbor
air. The promise of each printed word a held breath,
and all across the ground still there is the ash
of the old red light district. As the late arrivals sit
themselves down, we ready ourselves for the slow
exhalation. Every soul in the place ignorant of how fine
a memory this will be in all the hard years that followed.

Jimmy Tsang's

Some nights I would wait for take-out
just to sit at the bar and listen to Dean
Martin getting kicked in the head,
stealing glances at the loud families
pushing fried egg rolls and plates
of sweet and sour pork around the Lazy
Susan. The plates heaving with steam
imported from the Yangtze Valley.
The parents tired and angry, their kids
just awful. Jimmy sometimes ducking
behind the bar, the smile slashing
his face. The lottery drawing coming
on the tv, every one of us knowing
luck wasn't on the menu. The snow falling
out there on Centre Avenue could just go
ahead and swallow us all. Walking home
a neighborhood stray pauses, looks
me over. I take it as tenderness. A small
sign of affection before calling it a night.

Ode to Dr. Sestric's Office

Dropping hoists and rails
to the street, men perched
on the scaffold are loud
in their cursing. It's how
the terribly frightened say
'love'. Here the whole city
is pregnant. We rush
to replace our dead. We hold
to the sun as it rolls across
these snoring hills, take note
of names embroidered
on lamppost flags. The light is
waiting-room gray and somewhere
my heart falls down
endless flights of stairs.

Uneeda Biscuit

Snow falls in the street same
as some buildings fell –
with a clumsy flourish. No
one bothered noticing
the thud
hard as last night's crack-up.
What could I say
that the Uneeda Biscuit sign
hadn't already. All these years
standing here in every weather,
looking no different
than the weather.
I want the sun sailing
across my bare arms
in all seasons.
I want you with me,
too. Bracing hard
together against
this river
we run.

January

Ach, January you are
endless, a bottomless cup
I never ordered. Instead
I sit for what seems like years
wondering where my sandwich is,
when will my wife show?
The horror isn't all this
not knowing. The hard part
is always the certainty.
I know the ice won't melt.
No one will clean the floor
of this gray mud I track
behind me. Tomorrow
won't bring February to the door.
Just more January.
Doing its best
to convince
me it's what I deserve
and lately I can't help
but agree.

Sarah

Am I spelling that right?
Is there an 'h'?
It is just so necessary
when we say Hi, Hello
and How are you really?
Heart, too.
It's early still
and mornings do this to me.
Ask that I make my terms clearer.
Another cup of this coffee
and you'll hear the buzz.
My own heart, too.
An alarm in the blood.

Beer for Breakfast

Better to have beer for breakfast
than nothing at all.
A day this cold
demands a little something
in the engine.
Tracks of all sorts
zig-zag in the new snow.
The street is stitched
like so many old coats, tattered.
Together making one whole coat
that still won't keep out the wind.
Later it all melts,
dripping from the roof
in heaving sobs
and you, too
are crying in fits.
All damn day.
Not everyone is waiting for the thaw.
Some of us are not yet ready
for this earth, soft enough now
to dig, and the cruelty of it
taking our friend
down into itself
and returning only these
bits of green
as if that
was enough
to fill
this emptiness.

A Letter to Jeffrey Dunn 1/21/22

A week out from when
they'll cut this little cloud
from my eye
I take a second
cup of coffee just
to keep my hands
warm. The fire's out
and there's no hurry
to refresh the embers.
In the old days
I'd write you
a letter, but I don't
do that anymore.
I'll try a poem, but I'll cut
it short if it won't
click. What would you want
to know anyhow
that won't fit in
twenty or so short lines?
Jeff, what's more important
than the weather (damn cold)
and what I listened to
last night (Geza Anda's
recording of Mozart's Piano
Concerto no. 23,
the Adagio) while Anna
put our son to bed.
4 o'clock this morning
I had to carry him

back to his room
from the couch, discard
him in the still warm
sheets, and even though
he kicked and pleaded
I failed to understand
his fear, the nightmare
fresh as new oranges
on his breath.
The sun not even a whisper
and already, Jeff
I own a failure
I will carry right
to the end.

Paddy Cake

Monday morning means stale doughnuts
at the bakery. The old woman behind
the counter coated in icing sugar makes no
apologies for the way things are. Just as
the slush piled up outside the door more
resembles a crude photograph of smoke
than any relation to the clean idea of snow
this world insists always that we readjust
expectations, clear our collective throat
of all complaints. Somewhere God is
dealing out twenty dollar bills
from his steep green stack, money
landing everywhere but where it's needed.

Forgotten Works

Jeff, whatever happened to the Cat Table?
Was it gifted to Daniel, or was it Cressida?
Thick with feline languor and August
afternoons, I dream of it some nights.
And what of the rest? You left a bag
of poetry journals on my doorstep. Fondly
I fingered those Moody Street Irregulars,
and the others too sometimes scattered themselves
across my bed. There was that grousing stairway
that led us from one decrepit bookshop to the next.
Neither bothered with dusting or much in the way
of friendliness, but still my cash did go. And then you
too were gone into the tree-dense west. Changes fell
hard on us all. I can never remember when first
we were friends. Hey Jeff, this thing would boil
down to a fine whiskey I think. It will burn
all the way down, each little glass of it. I'll sit up,
watch the morning crack against these ugly
new buildings. I'll write again, too. Don't worry.
Next time those damn silly cats of yours slink
into the loose corners of my dreams this machine
will be at my bedside and ready. Ink brimming and all.

Poem for a Friend in February

Snow dusted down the street makes
the morning brighter than it is my eye
still sore from surgery doesn't take it
well I wish I stayed in what will my poems
do without me walk in one another's valences
make phone calls type long letters finish off
last night's wine and nap out here the sun
is going blinding and white as a new stove
I want to know what you would make
of this but you're not talking I'll wait
to hear how it went in court today hope
for the best we all fuck up it's true go ahead
look the day in its cold glowing eye we're not
getting younger are we maybe it's best not to
think too hard about anything what happens
to what we love when we are not around to hold
it close the days all fall around us sometimes
we get lucky and don't have to spend all
those tumbling hours alone let this poem be
a little luck in your pocket a little luck for us all

Tommy Flanagan Plays Billy Strayhorn's
Daydream, Tokyo, 2/15/75

Cheers to this glowing patch of Pittsburgh
landed in the Pacific by elegant
hands, the supple skyline
singular as the the ecstatic flash
we share exiting a dreary tunnel, now pinioned
here to these alert, satisfied ears.
7212 Tioga Street, Rear
is what we hear rumbling up from under
your left hand. Love surging in waves
whether rivers or no. There's a ghost
in the smoke, a soft giggle
outside a men's room door, and all
the time it is rising, bright wash.
I can imagine Murakami dropping his yen
at the door and here found that very first well
he wandered, darker than dark, and he called its mouth
my city. Far removed from Westinghouse
High here is the pride of Westinghouse.
It's February again. The ice now cracking
like some joke. I'm blowing a daydream
of steam into chapped hands near the corner
of Main and Howley. Issa wrote, Some can sing,
some can't. The snow drips hoarsely from the eaves,
but I can only hear Billy decked out in Tommy's
skin, such a sweet alive-ness dancing its way
out of this rundown dissolute winter.

City Steps 2/26/22

for Paola Corso

From here the brown ribbon of
the Allegheny looks muddy
as my thoughts. Early spring
and I see it's on the rise; all around
these steps rise, descend, crack
in half, shatter while the garbage
shines, mute in the sun. Auden wrote,
We must love one another or die
then told the world to forget
he said anything about it.
He understood bombs dropping
are less threatening than the soft
bare belly trembling in the cool
and heat, how a mouth naked
to possibilities undoes nations.
It's fear all the way down, I guess.
The sky is full of the stuff, too.
Auden said it was the most dishonest
poem he'd ever written. That's a damned
lie!, he said. We must die anyway.
From here Butler Street appears stretched,
chopped. Something like a border
braced against invasion.

Poem for Scott Silsbe

Mary Ruefle says, The poem is the consequence
of its origins. I'm thinking about that while
reading your new book, and the fact one
of your poems mentions Ruefle could be said
to be the origin of this poem, or maybe
it's the bright cold morning and the many things
I have to do today, each a beginning in its own right,
each a way of naming the day. I call today Laundry,
or Buy Groceries, or Sit Still and Stay Calm.
A joke that last one. Its true name, of course,
is Read Scott's Book. And what a fine soubriquet
it is. That's how it starts. Our first words
lay claim to the small world we know.
Could we not say, this life is the consequence
of our origins? Pittsburgh, Detroit, my father,
yours. All of what sets us in motion. I wish
these poems of yours would never end. I want
all my days spent like this. The words
on these pages as certain as mountains and stars,
their ephemerality impossible to contemplate
from here, looking as they do
like they should go on forever.

The Couple to Our Left

Maybe if the couple to our left
was not here I could better appreciate
the kindness of your silence, the immense
gift of your absence

of judgment, no less astonishing
than a hospital on fire,
the patients burning right there in
their hard beds, time melting to the wick

as more of the nameless go
up in smoke. Delirious and not a little strange

to consider it this way, how I feel
mornings with you, the last sticky bits of night
falling away from our suffering bodies
without sound, your eyes clear of sleep saying it all.

Coffee Cups from the Kitchen

It could have happened years ago now
or only a day, what felt then
endless as the fog green on the cathedral.
What we thought as forever

was a cloak obscuring the truth
of our interchangeability to one another

and how the days all dressed like one
another and the rain becoming snow
becoming afternoons in your bed, your parents
out and your dog asleep on the stair.

You carried coffee cups from the kitchen,
we read books and napped. Eventually
someone said it's time so we left it at that mistaking
languor for love, boredom for some deep kind of belief.

Scotty's Diner

I should go back again to Sunday mornings at Scotty's
Diner watching time stretch its silver wings
then decide, nah, better stay put; watch the pink Formica
go brown from the tramp of parking lot mud;
the slam of the cheap screen door and the line of growling
bellies testy outside, a serenade same as the steam
whistling up from the whole ham warming there; the fire
sparking with each spit of bacon grease, cartons of eggs
piled at the ready, and a bowl of melted butter brighter
than noon. Here is where I most felt alive. Even in
the tiny stinking men's room. Maybe she remembers,
too, how we couldn't help the happiness, and like
the older couples who brought the papers with them,
passing sections back and forth deftly as partners
in a long-running game of Hearts, we also exchanged
the news of the day, all of which appeared to us
in headlines of sky-high Helvetica – LOVE LOVE LOVE.

Roundabout Trace

for Don Wentworth

Don, it's raining again and that's just
as well. Someone on the bus said
something about angels and tears. Don,
no one was ever this sad, so torn-up
over how it is they wrung themselves
out like a lousy washcloth. It'll stop
soon, I think. Or it will go on
like this, never calling it quits.
The weather has sure got some stamina.
We blame climate change, but maybe it's
just the air and the oceans, and more
than all the rest it's the rain has had enough
of our bullshit and wants us to know,
Shape up or it's time for you to go.
Hey Don, I spend a lot of time trying
not to think this way. I feel better
when I hear a bit of Bach or Clifford
Brown. I feel like it's going to be okay
when I remember my copy of The Narrow
Road to the Deep North is waiting
by the bed. It's better, Don, when we share
a beer in any kind of weather. It's
a roundabout trace of the better life
we could have if each and every one
of us could stick a hand inside and shut
off the damn spigot. Just like that
it would be beautiful, the blood bright
on our raised fists, a sign we had the courage
to do the hard thing and show those angels
who we really are.

I Like It Here

I like it here
noisy as it is and filled
with people I do not like;
fraught with complications,
that's just how it goes.
Sometimes we get out
just the two of us,
somewhere we can get
a good look at one another,
breathe a little air finer
than in the city;
and there are days, too
when I can't bear
going anywhere.
I just want to be here,
alone will do,
but really it is so much
better with you. And yes,
sometimes we open
our eyes and here we are
yelling at each other,
walking away,
walking out,
but I like it here
and will always come back.
The sun marks the place
that makes my blood sing,
the wind and rain talking
behind my back, the sky

itself bending down
to whisper something
to a stranger, and here I am
because I like it here,
and I hope, dear
you like it here, too.

Poem

One more long
season slides
away, and love,
you tell me
we will find
ourselves
here again
lifetime
after lifetime
after lifetime
our scars
exactly
as they are
and the star-dazzled
night a thing
of shattered
beauty.
O love,
there at the end
of everything
what will
we say?

Kristofer Collins is the publisher of Low Ghost Press and the books editor at *Pittsburgh Magazine*. He is the co-host of the Hemingway's Summer Poetry Series. His most recent books include *The River Is Another Kind of Prayer: New and Selected Poems* (Kung Fu Treachery Press, 2019) and *Salsa Night at Hilo Town Tavern* (Hyacinth Girl Press, 2017). He lives in Pittsburgh, PA with his wife Dr. Anna Johnson and their children Cassidy and Joni.